Dreams and Metaphors

George Katkus

BookLeaf Publishing

Presentation by *BookLeaf Publishing*

Web: www.bookleafpub.com

E-mail: info@bookleafpub.com

ISBN: 9789357445214

First edition 2021

Change

Change is thick in the air I breathe
Things that I could never foresee
The break-up that tore me apart
Then a few friends tried to mend my heart

Surrounded in nature I decided on a second
change
I didn't know the decision would bring such pain
I decided to move still, to the town I said
I needed to let God know I wasn't dead

So I left the comfort I most needed then
Trying to reconcile my pain and sin
Struggling still to know what I need
Trying to look past two years of greed

The break-up is still most painful
The change that left me feeling shameful
Confusion came with it you see,
A question I ask won't let me be.

Did I do something wrong, did it have to
happen?
What was missing, was it passion?

That unanswered question will haunt me for a time
I lost so much, but once again found my rhyme

And leaving what I had for mere possibility
I thought I was strong, but it was just humility
Change is happening all around
A few make me smile, most bring a frown

It feels to soon to write of death
But whatever, I keep wasting my breath
I wish it was me so there'd be less pain
So other families wouldn't need to deal with the change

I wish it was me because I want to know if I made it
I wish it was me because I feel like I'm unfit
Not physically, I don't need to work out
But every other way I feel to weak to shout

I wish it was me because of everyone I've hurt
The good were taken instead and that's so much worse
I'm not trying to kill myself, I'm not suicidal
But "to die is gain" the words of Paul

The stress of life feels heavy today
I still feel hurt, no matter how much I pray

I don't want to hurt others so I remain pretty shy
It feels like I left without saying a proper
goodbye

This is what's in my mind, what you'll be getting
into
This might be news, but for others it's not new
I swear sometimes, but try to hold my own and
tongue
There's little left in me, but I'm not nearly done

I doubt myself a lot, you'll see
This is just to get you started on the real me
So enjoy the peek at my hidden mind
I write of good, but I'll show you another time.

Shattered Glass

Once upon a time I had a dream
Not the happy kind that makes you smile
But the depressing one that lasts for a while
One that makes wake up and scream

You were on a beach. We both were
I walked up to you, with a seashell
You said something to me, but what it was I couldn't tell
But from the faked smile I could tell something hurt

Then you walked away, as my hand was outstretched
Just then I shouted your name. Samantha. Please don't.
I tried to say it loud, but it was a whisper. Please don't.
And you just kept walking, until I was all that was left

Then I remembered what you said. "I must do this."
And I knew. You meant commit suicide.
You had to go away, to go and hide.

And leave our beach of bliss.

Then I was back again, at the beginning.
Unsure what to do, but trying to stop you.
Approaching now with wine by the ocean blue
And hoping that I could change the ending

We talked, and you listened. But I didn't understand.
"I still have to do this, I know it will hurt."
But why did you have to leave, and not put in work?
"Life isn't easy, but let me hold your hand."

"Goodbye. You tried so hard, but it's impossible."
And she left, my head low, her loss repeated
As I heard the wine glass shattering, my mind defeated.
And I just let you go, because in your mind, I am feeble.

Then it happened again, I was brought back.
"Stop trying to save me, use that energy for someone else"
But I had nothing else to do, life was a living hell
And I just let you go down that track

The wine glasses were both empty from the first moment
And we never even got to fill them with drink
And all I could do was negatively think
How much more could love show?

I woke up and screamed, lost all my sleep.
Realizing it was all just a dream, a projection of fears
But that doesn't mean you don't cry tears
I didn't know dreams could go that deep

Then, you actually walked away from me
While I was walking towards you, just like the dream
And you walked without purpose, at least it seemed
But now I know the things that could be

As for the dream, anytime someone dies
They leave me, a friendship lost for any reason
That's why I'm scared of this very season.
But fear is no longer a reason not to try

I had a dream my 2 best friends turned into teddy bears
That they were never able to come back to the earth
Now they no longer live in my mirth

And I slowly moved on until I didn't care.

I had a dream of my middle-school friends and ire
We were at my birthday party, they went to get drinks
Then something happened, I couldn't think
The sadness within was a depressing fire

They were all dead, their corpses in the freezer
I opened it, their heads all rolled out, holes in the middle
That was my first dream prophecy, the first riddle
On my head appeared a laser the size of a tweezer

Now my friend is the victim of another nightmare
I walk into the living room, she hangs by the fan
I do nothing but scream, and have no plan
These visions of mine aren't fair

I'll fight this one too, but even stronger than before
Because she is just a friend, family, after all
And I don't want her to be prey and fall
So I'll do whatever I can, no matter how sore

Shattered Glass happened in all the nightmares
The the freezer screen, the TV, the wine, the
lights
So maybe it's useless to really even fight
But losing her to sadness is beyond compare.

Shattered Glass, Shattered Glass, Shattered
Glass
You have brought nothing but eternal pain
We are nothing, we are not the same
I will finally leave you in my past.

Trying to Walk Away

When I tried
To walk away
You clung to my arm
Told me to stay
Because your pain
Won't go away
But when I'm here with you
You can make it through the day

If I want
To go somewhere
You hop in the car
Say you'll take me there
And our pains
Cannot compare
With the journeys we had
Everywhere

So when you went
To walk away
I clung to your arm
Asked you to stay

And my pain
Won't go away
But when you're here with me
I can make it through the day

If I want
To travel afar
It's so I can be
Where you are
And the pain
Has left us scarred
Oh why can't I be
Where you are

When we talk
From miles away
We still try to smile
Through the pain
And our hurts
Will fall like rain
Onto our skin
More and more everyday

Then you came walk-
ing back to me
A smile on your face
And tears on your cheeks
And said "sorry
But I can't let you be

Cause all that I want
Is you here with me"

"Because when we tried
To walk away
We clung to each other
In the pouring rain
Side by side
We'll walk again
Now and forever
Until the end"

A Broken Man

See before you a broken man
He once was whole, but now is not
He has only a face, and feet to stand
The rest is taken. Stolen then bought

See before you the same head.
It's ears and eyes are missing, only the tongue remains.
So he can longer rest in his bed
Because he gave too much with no self restrain.

See before you the same feet.
They are gone now, leaving only some toes.
Toes with which to to walk, as if to greet.
But filled with endless woes.

See the man, sitting, unable to cry
For his eyes are no longer working for him
And the man just tries and tries
But his situation grows ever more grim.

See the pain he carries day by aching day
Struggling at times just to live
He lives a life full of his own decay
And has no longer a reason to strive

See the man before you, broken.
The weight of his world on his shoulders
A man who is not heard when he's outspoken
A man not listened to by those who are older.

See a man before you, trying without reason
A man with despair that doesn't know to let go
He struggles and struggles, but then is accused of treason
As he faces things that very few know.

A man before you, just wanting normalcy
Will you try to give it to this husk?
He will thank you, amazingly, gorgeously
But no one can seem to smell his rotting musk.

The man before you howls in pain
But a sound does not escape his lips
For he has no lips to scream in the rain
And cannot warn the sailing ships

What has done this to the man?
What can bring one so durable to his knees?
It's because no one is willing to hold his hand
So he remains an outcast in the trees.

He searches for eyes and ears and body
But cannot find it with just his feet and tongue

But his tongue cannot recall the taste of strawberry
And has many songs left unsung

Song he no longer can sing anymore
Because he sounds not the same as remembered
He sounds deeper, more experienced than before
And no one recognized his face in September

They looked for the man they know as a child
The one who could sing and enjoyed life
The one who was crazy and wild
Not the one laden with strife

No longer accepted, they didn't see him.
He walked and shouted till he couldn't see himself
A shattered Glass once full to the brim
Possessing neither fame nor wealth.

Then he saw the monsters could be people too.
They act normal, but have false motive.
For those who do not recognize those who grew
Are themselves rotting and bloated

But they are loved, at least. By those around.
Which is more than what the man receives.
He remains run into the ground
Because he would not let himself be deceived.

The man looks at the crashing waves.
How much better would it be to simply drown.
But he has no lungs and makes no grave
For he will die without making a sound.

No splash, no effect on those who walk around
his corpse
His feet and tongue finally rot away too
All around him is the ever familiar Thorpe's
As unchanged in years as the ocean blue.

Dream

My chest feels your head
As my heartbeat silences your dread
Child, you can fall asleep here
Rest your body my dear.

Dream of the stars in the sky
Dream you're among them and can fly
Soar over the mountains and oceans
On wings that will never be broken.

Fly as far you can, feel the wind on your face
Watch the birds next to you prepare to race
The creatures below look at you in awe
As you're the most inspiring thing they ever saw

Or, if you will, dream that I'm with you.
That we're looking up at a sky so blue
That we're at a beach, on the cool sands
On sifting grains that won't stay in your hand.

Or dream that we're swimming in the sea
Floating, splashing, happy as can be
Gasping whenever a dolphin surfaces
As you realize that maybe life is worth it

Or dream that we're in a forest covered in green
The liveliest place you've ever seen
With deer running, and birds nesting
And both of us laying here, resting

Or dream that we're where we are
You leaning your head on my chest and looking at stars
And rest as I run my fingers through your hair
Rest, while we're out of the sun's glare.

Psyche

I don't believe in fairytales.
Not anymore, anyways.
I've been too much of a failure
To dream of the day.

I dream instead of an endless school.
Where kids are expected to reach the potential
set for them.
Where I was too busy to be cool
And all my problems stemmed

The g.p.a. given by the test had to be achieved
Or you would forfeit your chance in life
Was a lie I so easily believed
And it caused me so much strife.

The g.p.a. I needed to achieve in the dream
Was a five point five g.p.a.
But it's even more difficult than it seems
When it stayed at a two point eight

I was going to get kicked out of everything
Because of the unmeetable expectations
And I had nothing that I could bring
And no hope for salvation.

So I decided to just give in, and stop even trying
To live life as a fight to this lie
So it wouldn't matter much if I ended up dying
Because I would have been the only one to try

I know this boy was me in this nightmare
And my parents were the school that wanted the impossible
I know that I never had a single prayer
Of making their ridiculous expectations possible

They wanted me to be the best! The brightest!
But that's never been how they raised me.
I lost that the moment they put me through the test.
And now I'm something they'll never see.

I never wanted to be a scientist
I never wanted to be a mathematician
I never wanted to be forced into this
I never wanted to face their ambitions

I never wanted to play soccer
I never wanted to cross country run
I wanted to fill my life with happiness and laughter
And to write poetry under the sun

They punished me after forcing me to do sports
I wanted to join the chess club
And have fun and build forts
Not have my future snubbed.

Or the dream I had last night
The one where I could've given all for a woman
But ended up having to fight
And avenging many humans.

There was a killer in this one.
One who was never found
Me and my friends never run
So we started poking around.

My friend and I found a clue
And we started to investigate
He brought a crossbow along too
In case we needed it to be safe

Then I got knocked out
And woke up in a cave
There were people below
Who seemed to be safe

So I tried moving, but found no way down
And looked to the right and saw three areas of snow.
I had no idea the way to get back to town

And no idea if I could even go

I melted one, thinking only of escaping
It melted quick, I saw Christmas presents.
Just then I heard a scraping
And hoped it was someone I didn't resent

It was the woman I fell for
The one who had everything I liked in a female
Strength, ability, perceptive, not poor
Funny, smart, and good for the ails

"I saved you dummy! I got you these gifts!
And we can get married soon!
Let's open them before your mind shifts,
And we can decide who is the big spoon"

She moved closer to me, put my leg between hers
And started eating some bagels from a bag
I couldn't think of any words
So I just watched her eat and brag

I thought of kissing her, and I certainly tried
But in the end, she was too busy eating away
I felt like I could just die
And the mere touch of this beautiful lady

But I needed to see the other areas, so I melted it

The top one, I mean. To see just how many there were
No matter how prepared I was, no matter how much grit
I couldn't have been prepared for for what was unfurled

My friends head, sewed onto his own body
And several other people, with the same look
They were all terrified and made to be gaudy
Probably not knowing what was took.

"Save me, please, save me. AVENGE ME PLEASE!
That woman did this to us, it hurts
Please save us from the pain, so we can be at ease"
I was filled with emptiness, and something even worse

I was filled with sadness, anger, and rage
I knew I could not fight her normally
But I tried anyways, carrying their pain
And she just raised them up the ceiling stormily

And there they were electrocuted without mercy
"They're hurting because of you
Because you just had to try and finish this controversy

Now I'll shock them till I get what I want from
you!"

I had an idea, just then, listening to their screams
I would seduce her, then stab her in the back.
They didn't know that I carried a knife between
hidden seams
So it gave the perfect opportunity to attack

As I finished forming the plan, I woke up.
Bitter and nearly screaming in pain
And felt like such an empty cup
Like my head was full of rain

Every lover I've ever had has tried separating me
From those people I love, those I could get
closer
Or tried connecting me with failed family
And had been a sort of boaster

Maybe I'm not meant for love from my type
Maybe I need to stay away from those carnal
desires
And from people who build a fake hype
Just to hide what they conspire

These dreams told me who I am. Or who I was.
I don't reveal these two dreams very lightly
Nor do I open very much because

I don't like others seeing my psyche

Fire

I close my eyes as I feel this pain
I was a butterfly, with wings of flame.
The flame is dying, I need to sit down
My legs are too weak to carry me around

I tried to hold on to you and your hands
And the cold you brought I wanted to
understand
It turned the clouds to rain, which fell on me
Blinded my eyes so I could no longer see

It rained on my wings, which I couldn't protect
And started to weaken them, and make my hair
wet
Sitting in the rain, with no warmth from you
Your words colder than your eyes, which are
sometimes blue

I was powerful, before we met that day
And I should have known to stay away
We're too different, and it would never work
And left at least me feeling hurt

I wish I could fly on my wings again
But right now, I can't even stand

I pull my legs towards my chest, trying to keep warm
My legs and arms exposed to your storm

Then you walked away, and I eventually dried
But my flames were so weak I almost died
And I cried tears of flame onto my skin
Thinking about how you sinned

How you knew you would almost end my fire
How you didn't care, and just fed into your desire
You wanted my flame to make you thaw you out
But left me when you made my wings a drought

Turning my head in shame, that I ever fell for your lies
Wishing you would have let me say my goodbyes
Because you're the only one who had the strength to say yours
And left me getting weaker while the rain pours

My flame will come back though, it will take time
And I will not fall for the same crimes
For the wounds you have dealt to me before
For the way you made me weak and sore

I am powerful, beyond just my wings
And I am stronger than just my heat
You threw everything you had at my face
And I survived it all, you left your bitter taste

So I'll sit here, and regain my energy
I still cannot walk, and there is no remedy
But my wings will grow to fly me away
From the lies you told, and all of the pain.

And you had to walk away, because you were afraid to melt
Even more so afraid of what you might have felt
A longing, a caring for someone finally
But you were too afraid you would no longer be

Maybe someday, someone else will warm your heart
I tried, but you resisted and tore me apart
So someone someday will open your eyes
And you'll stop using other's to give you a prize.

Field of Black Roses

A field of roses, dark as they are beautiful
Finding it makes one feel weird
Honored, worthy in a way, almost, immutable
Like you have value, without being feared.

The rose petals ever so gently cause worry
As the dark harkens to a way of rebirth
They tell of the past, but not a journey
This beautiful rose of questionable worth

The thorns make sure to protect the rest
Sitting pretty to prick the wandering hand
Some still try to grip it, to take the test
And prove themselves worthy of rose so grand

The rose was not always black, it used to be
white.
The hand that is pricked bleeds into the roots.
To weed out the weak and deliver it's spite
To bring silent shame akin to a noose.

The roots absorb the blood and turn the rose red

Blood brings beauty and passion to whom it is given
Sacrifice and loss and painful dread
Are worth it to those truly driven

The blood dries in the petals, then turning black
Noting the finale of all sacrifice
Causing those who gave to wish to turn back
But those who receive to enjoy with their eyes

Black roses do not signal rebirth, denoting only death
And sacrifice, for a moment's lasting beauty
Roses each cost one breath
This field full of loss and duty.

A field of black roses, once a field of white
A land marred by too much pain
Even in the day, when all seems bright
Is not darkly beautiful as it is in rain.

Skeletons

Some people have skeletons in their closet
Some people try saying they have none in theirs
Some people say their problems fit in their pocket
Some say their problems start in a chair

I have no skeletons in my dressers
That's because I am one, covered in flesh
And often it makes me feel lesser
Piloting this meat skin, no longer fresh.

But I'm ok with being a skeleton. I am the story.
The story of what I have been, and my growth.
Between muscle and skin is veins of glory
The silent rushing keeps on to fulfill an oath

My heart is in my ribcage, prison bars for emotions
And it's trapped by me, but keeps me alive too.
I have never seen such a poisoned devotion
When my own hearts starts bleeding through.

And my brain is held even tighter than my heart

It's surprising that it's still able to serve it's purpose
But then it tells me, silently, that even with what I start
I will never be anything more than worthless.

And my eyes, they see the world, but has no way to be free
As they are held in place, teased and hurt by the light
Sometimes I force it to look in the mirror, at me
And hope that it likes the sight.

The rest of the body was easy to control after that
Because everything it is ties back to those things
And so sometimes I feel a bit mad
And don't know what darkness I will bring.

So I am a skeleton, welcome to my life!
I just want to show you what's really true.
To show you how I bring myself strife
And wonder, are you just a skeleton too?

Ataraxia

In Collab with Sonakshi

Lying here in your arms, cares fade away,
like the ash after wood is exposed to flame.
The warmth you bring are coals for the heart,
the fire reflected in your eyes is a work of art.

You caress my face, as I fall asleep,
my worries and thoughts now buried deep.
Your hazel eyes flicker like those stars,
which shine brighter just to hide my scars.

Lying here with my lover, my flame, my heat,
the look in your eyes makes my heart beat.
I dream of us in this peaceful moment,
two lovers whole, never to be broken.

I dream of us basking in pure bliss,
your treacherous lips, I long to kiss.
Instead, I prefer your strong embrace,
for you are my haven, my safe solace.

Your touch brings an energy and indescribable
peace,
it drives me crazy, yet gives me release.

As if you're both a poison, and the medicine I need,
I feel unrestricted while I follow your lead.

You're all I need, to retain my sanity,
an irreplaceable soul in my closest memories.
Lying in your arms, I see a raging fire
that emanates from us, our love's desire.

The flame dances and mimics our lips,
a burning passion, the world is eclipsed.
The warmth in your touch shows the heat of your passion,
the need of our hearts spurs us to action.

Our deeds are needs that our hearts fulfill,
your sizzling touch brings time at standstill.
You look at me lovingly, embracing my soul,
just how the horizon kisses the shore.

See the need in my eyes, they hunger for your taste,
your lips, your mouth, your tongue, your pining embrace.
Like the waves meet the sand, our lips do too,
kissing you slowly in waves, enjoying our youth.

Desire flickers in your eyes, as I awaken to reality,

Lying in your arms, I replay the dream's brevity.
Calmness washes over me, as I feel your heart beat,
My soul smiles at this moment, trapped in relief.

Lying here with you, the world passes us by
As we finally fall asleep in each other's eyes
Ataraxia, calmness unlike any other could bring
Two souls in harmony like a gentle stream

Night Sky

A vast expanse
I cannot reach
Or use my hands
But I can see
The stars up there
They're oh so clear
I stop and stare
Release my fears
There's so many
Too many for numbers
The amount aplenty
Those burning wonders
I'd almost forgotten
What they look like
How much I wanted
To revel in the sight
My mind strays
From normal thoughts
Fears betrayed
Joy has been caught
Oh star, oh stars
Reach down to me
I can see where you are
Bringing light to my feet
A pale light

But it's bright still
I get lost in the sight
As you bring back my will
Oh wonderful night sky
Filled with nuance and color
You've never denied
The beauty of summer

Letting go of the winters
When you were always there
I think of it and shiver
How little some people care
But I'm working on letting go
Letting go of the lies and hate
Even if I have to go where I don't know
Even if I'm a little bit late
I'm letting go of the unfilled promises
Letting go of the years of pain
Letting go of self-hate that kept me from being honest
Letting go of the negativity of rain
Letting go of unmet expectations
Letting go of what holds me back
Letting go of my desperation
Letting go of this life turned black.
Looking at the sky, I see it all
Nothing is forever, not even pain
Life is just one constant free-fall
If you stress you won't stay sane

But if you relax, comfort follows
As if falling was the same as flying
My pride is too big to swallow
But I'm working on it, lost in the night sky

Into the Arms of Nothingness

I run into the arms of nothingness
And find nothing but all of us
The people who lost, or will lose
The whole of humanity has been used

Taking steps forward, though we don't know where
Removing all obstacles from our path, even our hair
Not understanding our impending doom
that'll no doubt come pretty soon

Though none of us will live to die that day
Or maybe we will, we're stuck in place.
Our life isn't flashing before our eyes
What flashes instead is those we despise.

Those who hurt the group that we're part of
Those who abandoned what's good for a false love
Those who would forsake all else but their life

Those who do what they think is necessary, and
cause strife.

But none of us will live to the day all is lost
So why act like our lives are too great a cost?
If you've never seen the view from a mountain
top
It's beautiful and terrifying enough to make you
stop

But if you fall, what then?
All your dreams suddenly somehow end.
But it was all worth it for one moment of clarity
For one second without a shred of despair to see.

So live your life for the beauty, climb that
danger
Live life with happiness, sadness, peace, and
anger
We're meant to feel all these things while we live
And understand these are meant to give.

Join me in the arms of nothingness
And see that life is filled with sadness and bliss
If we're meant to die, let's feel it all
And experience every emotion before mankind's
fall.

Flooding

Shuffling my feet slowly on the path
Poor little stream beside, feel the dam's wrath.
Flooding slowly, wetting the bottom of my shoes
A rope around the land's neck that'll never get
loose.

Leaves once dry now start to get wet
As water and leaf have finally met
Water rises slowly, to the top of the leaf
Signaling the end of all relief.

Things on them start to die on the ground
Bugs in silent pain as they cannot make a sound
The water had risen to the top of the rubber on
my shoe
It's rising faster than thin bugs knew.

It rises a little more, I see my cat coming out to
me
A faithful companion that won't let me be
The water is up to it's stomach now
I cry a little as it just says "meow"

Picking him up, I'm wishing life wasn't this way

I wish we could be together forever, and never go away.
I think I've finally got a name for him, bombă
A name both beautiful, and quite a bit somber.

Running back home, water up to my shins
Wanting to see Mom and Dad again
Home is a bit far, the water is up to my ankles
But I'm at the front door just beside the stable

"Mom! Dad!" I shout out inside the house
The few chairs now empty, things quite as a mouse
The water's risen to the seats of the chairs,
I grab one and start taking it upstairs.

I should be safe for an hour with bombă here
But I don't want mommy and daddy to dissapear
I look into my cat's eyes, and take note of the green
If not for our imminent demise, we'd've made a good team

The water is again at my feet, and I start to panic
Whoever set this up is a painful maniac
It rises to my ankles, and I don't know what to do
I just want bombă and I to look at the sky and its blue

Up to the shins, I cannot think
I want to escape before I can sink
Up to the knees, and my mind fights itself
It's tearing itself apart and ignoring health

Up to my waist, and I feel so lost
Holding bombă to my chest, my body is
exhausted
It rises further to my stomach and bellybutton
I want to survive, but I can do nothing

It rises to my chest, and I hold bombă up above
it
I put him on my head, and he just started to sit
"I love you, my best friend. Maybe you can
survive.
But I can't, I think I'm going to die."

"Please live, since I won't be able to
I want one of us to make it through."
The water's up to my chest, breath quickens
"Mommy? Daddy? I wish you could listen.

I can't be strong, I said I wouldn't shed a tear
But mommy and daddy, you left me alone here."
The water's up to my neck, and I can hardly
breathe.
"Bombă, please remember me."

He meowed in response, then jumped off.
And swam through the window and couldn't be stopped.
I cried as the water covered my mouth and nose
The last thing I'd see was watching him go.

The water is over my eyes and I close them instinctively.
I have a minute left before breathe leaves me
I open my eyes to see a flash of light
Then a wave of destruction that I can't fight.

My Best Friend

I'm talking to my best friend
One I met so many years ago
I thought by now our relationship would end
But I'm happy it stayed though

My best friend knows all about me
Has been there through the best and worst
We talk about pretty much everything
Including how I've been blessed and cursed

We also talk of how I've been hurt, and healed
How relying on other can be good sometimes
In fact, it's because I talk that my wounds are
repealed
And I can easily rest my own mind

This one is special. But parents never thought
so.
They never supported me talking to you.
They always seemed to expect you to go.
But you've been a friend most true.

And they can't take credit for our friendship
So they don't talk of you to others at all

But still people see us and support our relationship
Understanding that you've kept me from many a fall

You were there through all my romances
Through my fake and real friends as well
You've heard of all my dances
And there's nothing that you'll tell

You know every lake I've been to so far
And every ocean I've seen in life
You've seen all of my scars
And have been there through every strife

Finally writing a poem to you, it feels nice
Like a breeze on a cool evening
Like the happiness and joy felt by mice
And you've helped me move past my grieving

Thank you for sticking by me, even if you didn't have a choice
Thank you for listening and helping me understand my thoughts
Thank you occasionally being my words and voice
Thank you for helping me understand what I sought

This one is for you. My most cherished perhaps
The one who always has me on hooks
The one who can read me like a map
Thank you, my best friend, my notebook

Depression

Maybe depression isn't what you think
Maybe darkness isn't what you feel
It comes and goes before you blink
Like some kind of messed up seal

Maybe depression is feeling sad without a
reason
Maybe depression is inability to give the proper
response
Maybe depression comes and goes with the
season
Maybe it's something you don't feel all at once

Maybe depression is not smiling during a
beautiful day
Maybe depression is suddenly slowing down
when you walk
Maybe depression is not knowing how to pray
Maybe depression is not knowing when to talk.

Maybe depression is different for each
individual
Maybe depression is something more common
yet less
Maybe depression is something openly personal

Maybe depression isn't actually caused by stress

Maybe depression just does what it pleases
Maybe depression doesn't care if now's a good time
Maybe depression is like a paper with creases
Maybe depression blurs out those important pencil lines

Maybe depression is had by someone close
Maybe depression is something that can't be avoided
Maybe depression, for no reason, makes you feel morose
Maybe depression tells you you're only useful to be exploited

Maybe depression is caused by a past action of someone else
Maybe depression has no purpose or reason, yet is there
Maybe depression has a hidden meaning, has mastered stealth
Maybe depression latches on to anyone, rude or fair.

Depression is worse than feeling lonely, it's feeling alone
It's feeling by yourself while surrounded at home

Depression isn't feeling like you're enough
It's feeling useless, not just feeling rough

Depression is something that you only
understand with experience
Depression is something you can't take from
others
Depression is feeling like your siblings aren't
sisters nor brothers
Depression is a mist to all, only to some it's
mysterious

I just got off a 3 week depression, here's what it
looked like
The world was fine, and I was alright.
But when I wanted to write, I couldn't lift my
pen
When I wanted to talk, I didn't know what to say
and when

When I wanted to help my friends, I had no
strength
Desire, ability, knowledge, and power, I had
those at length
But all in all, I had no way to be strong
And I worried for so so long.

Worried about the past, about my failures
About things I missed as child that just leer

Worried that the mistakes I made made me
unworthy
Worried that if I was perfect, I'd never be hurting

I knew the right words, but couldn't say them to
myself
I listened to the sky, but never felt God in myself
I cared for others, but didn't know how to care
for me
Even though I'd done it before, I felt like I didn't
deserve it, see?

I missed the days when I didn't know I was
missing guidance
I missed the days when I was blissfully in the
audience
The days that I didn't realize I was robbed of
knowledge
The days before I realized life is more than just
college.

The days I looked forward to things, they're
mostly gone
Now I just look forward to dinners with friends
and a free dawn
I find no enjoyment in looking at the past
Only tears in my eyes, wishing the good could
last

That was my depression. And more still.
Like thinking I was never enough, like I have no will.
Not enough for those who were supposed love me the most.
Not enough for those friends I lost like an unknown ghost

I moved past my fears of shattered glass
But those shards still hurt, even from the past
The wounds never festered, but I was still infected
I left life on the shelf, and it came back different from how I left it

But as you can see, I can write again
My mind has started to once again mend
I cannot control it. But I have survived every depression.
So I took this chance to teach the doubters a lesson.

Depression will never go away as long as I live
But that doesn't mean I'll just give
Depression is not a choice, it is a reality
But I have stood with others as they've stood by me.

Criterion

What's the criteria for respect?
It used to be angels and kings and God and prophets
But now the angels have been treated with neglect
They can deal and survive, but who would want it?

The kings all have died and are seen as evil
For things they didn't know were going to hurt others
And if we're keeping things real
If you're reading this then you're rich as a king's mother

And God, we don't put anything in his hands anymore
People try to do everything with humans themselves
Which means they cry and cry till their throat is sore
But there's only one doctor for our spiritual health

"Vengeance is mine" says the Lord
But we stopped hearing his voice long ago
I wished pain on others once, and it hurt my words
It made me bleed and left me with nowhere to go

Since then, I've promised God I would always get back up
I would always go back to Him and trust Him
And He filled me to the brim like a kingly cup
And saved me from the eternal consequence of sin

The prophets were God's messengers in man
And yet many were not seen through kind eyes
Though most offered an extended hand
Many people accused them of lies

They spoke out against "religion" and "politics" when those were false
They were stalwart yet faltered when it came to death
And everyone knew what God could do, what's at God's call
That he could convert nations with just a breath

But as sexual freedom came, faith started to die
There were prostitutes in his temple.

THERE WERE PROSTITUTES IN HIS HOUSE. That's no lie.
If that were mine, I'd have burned it all.

Now we idolize humans, and not God who made them
Martyrs and living and those who think a certain way
We are all called to love God, both women and men
But we lost that love along the way

God is that love with which we should love Him
Yet there seems to be so little of it being shown
When the whole world seems dark, scary and grim
Just how much of God do you really know?

Do you think He agrees with everything you think?
You'd be wrong if you said yes to that
The Pharisees followed the law to the brink
But Jesus still reprimanded them, and that was that

In the face of perfection, they still got it wrong
So what makes you think Jesus wouldn't chastise you?
Of all the things he said, and every song

You must understand He decides what it means
to be true

That's all that matters. That's how you get
respect.
By throwing away your pride and thanking God
for giving you loved ones
And He'll just keep loving, He won't relent
He's in it for you, it's probably not for fun

The kings, the prophets, the jesters, the bards
The men, the women, the far and the near
The newborns, the middle aged, the ones we call
old farts
The enemies, the friends, and all those we hold
dear

The presidents, the teachers, the restaurant
workers
The customers, the sizers, and the cobbler down
the road
The police, the artists, the musicians, the janitors
The ushers, the actors, the one driving a
dump-truck load

The white, the black, the Egyptian
The natives, the visitors, the travelers
The African, the European, the Asian

The indigenous, the settlers, the ones who feel like they don't matter

None of these can escape from God's words
No one can truly be perfect except for Jesus
But when He speaks, it's like he's not heard
And we wonder why he's in no rush to meet us

Why meet with someone who only believes conveniently?
If they doubt you exist, they'll just make excuses
He could appear before you immediately
And you would still hear his words, but refuse him.

That's the cold reality, we don't recognize Jesus anymore
The martyr who took on a weight greater than the world
We live so fast and then get so bored
Look where the news was 3 weeks ago, and realized it's whirled

Stay still for a moment, try to remember what God looks like
They say it's impossible, but I was a kid one time
And I could see his face then, I could've said what it looked like

I could've explained all the details, colors, and lines

Maybe I was wrong, but God looked like a child's image of perfect
And now I can't understand perfection, or God, like I used to
But I still keep trying, because that knowledge must have been worth it
I knew what God looked like when I was a kid, I swear it's true.

What's the criteria God has to fit before you recognize him as such?
An all powerful being who fills your every want?
A God who agrees with you and is never too much?
How can creation decide what's God based on our criterion?

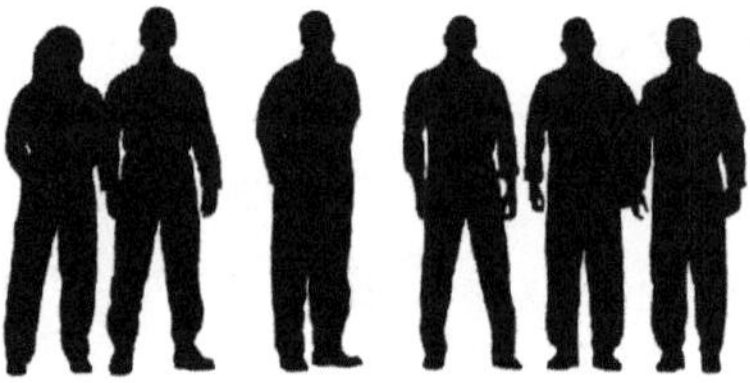

Waves

Waters roll and ebb and flow, motion is constant
Alive and blue, breathing, pushing pulling
Vivacious and momentous, beauty in the deep
Ever changing, ever moving, never sleeping
Shaming all who think they can overcome nature

I Wish

I want to walk along the beach with you as the sun sets
Watching the waves push and pull and hope our eyes met
To be held onto as we traverse the sands
Or to be blushing and holding your hand

I want to lay down on a hill after a picnic
Just side by side, our hearts racing quick
Maybe look over to you, instead of the falling sun
Our blood pumping louder than a gun

Then just holding each other in our arms for a while
Watching the stars, the dim blue light hiding our smiles
Eyes closed, my chin on top of your head
We'd fall asleep with only pointy grass for a bed

Life isn't so bad when I imagine us like this
You and I feeling some feeling of bliss
I'd like to walk the sands of life with you
And rest on a hill while the sky is blue.

We'd be honest and open, and fight sometimes
But come back to each other, I'd be yours and you'd be mine
And we'd laugh about how dumb that argument was
And find more comfort than ever in each other's hugs

I'd like to see the best and worst you could ever be
And be the reason you'd be so fun and happy
I'd like to see your depression, and be beside you throughout
And whisper support, and help banish your doubts

I'd like to see you and me grow with God together
And to walk towards Him now and forever
I'd like to see the parts of you that are Him
And to love you through both righteousness and sin

I'd love to see your smile, and know why you do so
I'd love to see your blush as you turn your face and go
I want to see your bashfulness, your shyness
To learn both your confidence and highness

I want to be with you, more than anything
And to be immersed in your life from spring to spring
I want to walk life's journey's with you by my side
And to share all our experiences on life's wild ride

Sensory Overload

These walls aren't soundproof, I can hear everything
One roommate watching tiktoks, another watching a movie
One does dishes, the one on tiktok is singing
And all of these sounds are too much for me

When I was with my sister and brother-in-law
And their children, age 4 and newborn
I never got confused by what I heard or saw
Despite there being more noise as I was worn

But the sounds of my roommates just keep changing
They're restless and have nothing to do, no purpose to fill
So they do many things, the sounds keep rearranging
As I am forced to suffer, too weak to fulfill my will

This is exhausting. Being with people, doing nothing of note
Filling the time with trying not to get angry
Filling my mind, hoping it's not broke

But these roommates all suddenly seem so mangy.

This is not me mad, it's me realizing the world is empty
Driven by politics, by games, by movies, by television, and media
People being driven to being resenting
And ignoring actual issues that plague us more, like lukemia

What can I do to heal this ill world, it's too comfortable to heal
Or change my roommates, or at least make them listen
Not many see these problems, or how to deal
If we could just shut all this off, humanity would glisten.

One More Dance

Smooth skin and deep oceanic eyes
Sparkling with clarity and pleasured surprise
Watching you dance I crack a smile
And think how I'd like to stay here a while

The joy in your movements and beauty in your feet
The crowd around looks up from their seat
Hair flowing in the gentle wind of the night
You look at me and wink with a smile of delight

Those cherry red lips are just a visage
For the kind soul you are, while the crowd applauds
The passion I see is too good to to be true
But then I see the lake and the moon

The poem I write is the dance that you dance
A passion, a desire, and way to make life last
So much time and effort, and a resounding art
Something people can look at and remember in their heart

I don't understand what you say with your body

Whether it's of life or forests or something naughty
But I understand the heart you've given
And the fire you make that keeps you living

When the night is done and the performance is over
I'll take you home before it gets any colder
We'll talk and I'll listen and try to understand
And when we get home, dance with you in my hands

I've been there for you since the day you were born
And I'll be there the day we are torn
But for now, let me try to dance with you again
To love how you love and joke about when you were 10

I won't have all the time, mine is slowly fading
So let me be with you and we'll do some trading
You teach me to dance, and I'll teach you to rhyme
Then we can love each other every time

Then I can part and dance with you at your wedding
And watch your beauty again as the sun is setting

I ask that you visit, and maybe we can dance and write
And I can see my grandchildren laugh and learn what's right

I told myself "one more dance" before 2 dances more
But now I'm wishing that I had done at least 4
I hope you teach your son and daughter to dance
I hope you teach them how to write and how to make plans

I hope you love in the ways they love you
I hope I guided you to a love that is true
I hope you know you're as beautiful as your mother
I know you danced with me like no other

A Thief on the Shore

I swear I saw a girl by the lake
She was just a silhouette, a shadow
Haunting ever closer, there is something she will take
She can come as close as she likes, with a river's flow

There is nothing in life I can't live without
I can still dream and pursue till I'm content
"Don't be scared, come closer!" I now shout
All things fade, she's scared but won't relent

I wonder what she'll take from me today?
Maybe she'll join me and I can give her a gift
Maybe she'll sit down and we can talk, I pray
Maybe she'll be filled with joy and her fear will sift

I have no reason to treat her with kindness
She took that from me a long time past
Though she took my eyes, she took also my blindness

I hope that when she takes she will never take
her last

She is not kind, but she is not at all cruel
I just wish she'd stay with me a while
She's never made me feel a fool
Sometime ago she took away my pride

I know she is coming. I've prepared for her
I've put everything I can on display
I can't see, but heard her say "sir!
Can I stay a while, and share with you my day?"

www.ingramcontent.com/pod-product-compliance
Lightning Source LLC
Chambersburg PA
CBHW051734130826
49812CB00033B/856
9789357445214